No
Gravity

Rudy Francisco

Cover Art: Artof Andres

Ingredients

Page

Broom

Sometimes, I'm the mess.
Sometimes, I'm the broom.
On the hardest days,
I have to be both.

Tremble

During an earthquake,
some will catapult
toward the nearest exit,
some will find a doorway
or crawl underneath a desk
and wait for the ground
to be comfortable where it unfurls.
The latter, is how the patient survive.

You
are full of tectonic plates
that aren't afraid of shifting.
Be careful of those
who fear your quiver.
They will cower at
the tremble of you.
They will run when the hands
of right now aren't so gentle
and loving
is an act of bravery.

Gum

For some people,
the word "Love"
is just chewing gum.
It's not food.

They like the way it tastes,
the way it masquerades
behind the teeth,
the way it burrows into
the tongue and sits there,
the way it fills the mouth
with flavor that has
no intention of staying.

They can spit it out,
leave it wherever it lands
and proceed
without a flinch.

Sea

Today,
I am just a sea
trying to make peace
with all the wreckage
inside of its stomach.

Hoping someone
will accept me,
broken ships
and all.

30/30 Horizon

I hope I haven't already driven
past my greatest moments.

I hope there is something
beautiful in the horizon
that's just as impatient as I am.
Something so eager,
it wants to meet me halfway.
A moment that is diligently
staring at its watch, frustrated,
bursting at the seams
and wondering what's taking
me so long to arrive.

29/30 Baltimore

I heard the city had been
on fire
for a while,
but now it has flames
to prove it.
The news said "Riot."
Personally, I think
it was more
smoke signal.

28/30 Skin

This skin says,
you better put on some lotion,
says, Jergen's is godly,
ash is of the devil
and Satan ain't winnin today,
says, don't use nothing on me
that doesn't have butter in the title,
says, if it can't stick to the wall,
it has no business being on this body,
says, Vaseline is a back up plan
and baby oil is the last line of defense,
says, don't forget the elbows,
says, don't forget the knees
says, don't forget all the spaces
in between the fingers,
says, pay attention.

Pay attention.

Says, if nothing else,
today,
we will shine.

27/30 PM

I usually wake
up at noon.
I shed sleep like
the rind of tangerine,
peel myself out of bed
and carve my initials
into the day around 12 :10.

I wonder if the morning
notices my absence.

26/30 Stardom

They say,
you are nobody until
somebody kills you.
Everyday, it seems
there is a new officer
dedicated to
making one us famous.

When we said,
we wanted the world
to know our names,
this isn't what we meant.

25/30 Hourglass

If I'm lucky enough to be
introduced to old age,
someday, my voice will be
a rusty hammer with no handle
and my hands will quake the way
any building does when it's
erected next to a train track.

I'll be the fog that
clings to the mirror
after the kind of shower you
take when the days are long.
I'll dissipate slowly.

If I'm lucky, this is
how the movie ends.
I'm not foolish enough
to ask God to put my
hourglass on its stomach.
I know all of this sand is
determined to reach the bottom,
but while I'm here,
I want to create something
that will last so long
it will look at my flesh
and laugh.

24/30 Thief

This body
is a glass house
that has swallowed
too many heirlooms.
Some days, I stare
at it in the mirror.
This is more stakeout
than admiration.

I am trying to find
new ways
to break
into myself.

23/30 Drive

Tell me a story
and let's laugh like it's the only
thing keeping us alive.

Play a song
and give the stereo
permission to use its
outside voice.
Let's sing loudly,
off beat and out of tune.
Let the world know
we don't care how it sounds
because the only key we need
is in the ignition.

Let's just go.
Drive until our troubles
phantom in the rearview mirror
and we forget they exist,
at least
for a moment.

22/30 Daylight

Once,
death was just a distant relative
we only heard stories about.
Assumed if we avoided stray bullets,
we'd never stand face to face
with this member of our family.
We were the black box on the airplane.
A story made of Kevlar and steel.

Now,
we forget things
and our bones are beginning
to sound like the floorboards
of a house that isn't
worth remodeling.

Mortality is a sunset
in slow motion
and we have so much to do
while there is still daylight.

21/30 Full

"Yea, that's my food.
You can have it."

This is how I love.
I barter what I own
and exchange it
for your happiness,
hoping it's enough
to make you full.

20/30 Speak

Most of my childhood,
I spoke with a stutter.
My mouth and mind
were 2 people
with no rhythm
trying to teach
each other how to dance.

I had to concentrate
to say the simplest things.

When there is struggle
in the veins of
every word,
you understand
that speaking is a
badge of honor
that some of us
have to fight for.

19/30 Birthmark

My skin
is a birthmark
I have learned
to wear proudly.

18/30 Venom

My biggest mistake
was pretending
you weren't poison.

It's easy to forget
even venom looks pretty
in good lighting.

17/30 Photograph

A man who doesn't feel
is just a photograph.

He's an
immature Polaroid,
a thousand words
trapped in the belly
of a dead language.

16/30 Black Emoji

Today,
for the 1st time,
I used the dark skinned
emoji hand.

She says,
why are you so angry?

I replied,
...I was just waving.

It's almost funny
how we assume
everything black
looks hostile.

15/30 Magic

My room is
a farm full of shadows.

Every morning,
the sun grows hands
and plucks every
strand of darkness
from the walls.

This is the only
sorcery I've ever
seen up close.

Today,
getting out of bed
is a magic trick
I'm still learning
to perform correctly.

14/30 Cigarette

You are a memory
flavored cigarette,
I know the dangers
of 2nd hand smoke
and I've never been
a big enough tray
to hold all your ashes.

13/30 400 Miles

We are beautiful
whenever we have
400 miles of
silence between us
and who we've become
stops interrupting
who we were.

12/30 Brother

When I call
you brother,
it means you have
at least 4 fists
during any fight
you can't talk
yourself out of.

11/30 Hunted

When they say he's black,
when they say he was unarmed,
when they say he was killed,
when they say the officer's name,
when they show his face,
when the system
licks his hands clean,
when they say there is no crime
on his fingers,
you realize the phrase
"Life is short"
sounds a little different
when you're being hunted.

10/30 Vacation

I imagine,
her smile is where
God goes on vacation
when our prayers
get overwhelming.

9/30 Grease Fire

Divorce is a stubborn grease fire;
a salivating mouth that still holds
an appetite after the kitchen
has been swallowed.

2 years ago, I watched this
greedy inferno steal the
wedding ring off
my mother's finger.

To this day, there is still
a relentless shadow on her hand.
The teeth marks of a
30-year promise left on a stove
that we all thought was turned off.

8/30 Gravity

The first time
I heard my name
in your mouth,
the ground felt like
a language I haven't
spoken in years.
I forgot everything
I knew about gravity.

7/30 Flock

Dear self,
today, your laugh is a
wild flock of wind chimes.
It exists the way happiness should,
feral, loud,
and allergic to apology.

6/30 Brick

I'm learning that
everything doesn't
always come back
the way you send it.
Sometimes, love
is more brick and
less boomerang.

5/30 Privilege

Privilege
is the ability to forget
there are places
where poverty
is the only thing
that isn't struggling
to stay alive.

4/30 Today

Today,
your face is more
kitchen than hallway,
your eyes are
2 stubborn faucets.
and running is their
only hobby.

Today,
right now is a
multiple choice question.
A, B, C say "Have a breakdown"
D is "All of the above."
Just do it.

When you find yourself
laying in a shatter
that could make a
windshield cringe,
don't scrap
the serial numbers
off your masculinity.

No one is coming
to take it back.
It's yours.
Just let go.

3/30 For J Dilla

Legend has it,
when J Dilla was admitted
to the hospital for the last time,
he brought his production equipment
and made instrumentals out of everything
in his body that wasn't ready to die.
The last thing he did on this earth
was make music.

How beautiful it is
to grind yourself into sand,
offer the grain of you
to anyone willing to listen.
Hoping they will carry your debris
into places you'll never go.

2/30 Sinking

I held you
the way a boat
holds water.
I always felt
us sinking.

1/30 Museum

When you choose to be a poet,
when you choose to spill like this,
bleed like this, cry like this,
your pain becomes an exhibit.
A place for people to walk through
and then leave when they are ready.
No one ever asks a museum
if it's doing ok.

I'm still
learning
to love
the parts
of myself
that no one
claps for.

Made in the USA
Columbia, SC
21 May 2020

97997462R00024